testimony

a collection

Paul Robert Mullen

testimony

a collection

Paul Robert Mullen

Coyote Creek Books | San José | California

Copyright © 2018 by Paul Robert Mullen

All rights reserved. No part of this book may be used or reproduced by any means, graphic, electronic, or mechanical, including photocopying, recording, taping or by any information storage retrieval system without the written permission of the publisher except in the case of brief quotations embodied in critical articles and reviews.

Names, characters, places and incidents are documented fictitiously. Any resemblances to actual persons, living or dead, events, or locales are purely coincidental.

Printed in the United States of America

ISBN-13: 978-1-946647-15-3
25 24 23 22 21 20 19 18 17   1 2 3 4 5 6 7

Cover design © 2017 by Jan McCutcheon

Published by Coyote Creek Books
www.coyotecreekbooks.com

*for those who lie awake
so their dreams have to wait*

also by Paul Robert Mullen

curse this blue raincoat (2017)

contents

one: prelude
motive — 3

two: fallen man
sometimes — 7
guilt — 8
eternal sin — 10
on breaking you — 11
one-woman-man — 12
sorry — 19
total control — 20
encore — 21
remedy — 22
in the end — 23
don't be surprised — 24
the fear at the back of my mind — 25

three: female of the species
in time — 29
Shakespeare wrote the most notable tragi-comedy — 31
dream catcher — 43
subtle rubble — 44
requiem for the lovers — 46
seasons — 53
separation — 55
don't — 57
you — 59
childhood — 64
the worst night of my life — 66
little joan — 70

infatuation   72
departure   73

four: temporary lights
return of the muse   77
long after the war   78
shall i do it anyway?   79
voodoo sound   80
call it wonder   81
i am not alone in this battle   82

five: street life
aftermath   87
on donald trump   94
vanity   95
death of society   96
whoever keeps taking them took him too   97
a mediocre journey   98
street life   101

six: spinning crimson
welcome the morning   105
hindsight   107
sunlight on the windscreen   108
avalon revisited   110
making the grade   112

seven: follow me
the reasons   117
my only idea   119

eight: curtain call
conviction   123

one

prelude

motive

some people think my poems
are full of pessimism
and misery
but
these people
are failing to really see
what's going on here

i'm not writing for them
i'm not writing for you
i'm not writing to win awards or grease my pole
get rich
        or get even

i'm writing
to get this monkey off
        my back
though it keeps jumping on
clinging
twisting
pulling me down by the throat

        the little *bastard*

two

fallen man

sometimes

i
want to climb
out
      of my bones

so nobody can see me

and rest
      for just a minute
in
the shadows
of
      my days

guilt

you gave me your heart
in a
      brown paper bag

told me to keep it
forever

instead
i smashed it to
smithereens

trampled it
like a feral elephant

crushed it
as though i was a satellite
plummeting
      to earth
      and you were underneath

i deserve nothing
from you
      but
the

       worst of you
and yet
all you ever give to
this
       fallen man

is love

eternal sin

i
always
get myself into this
         situation . . .

loved
      by those
i
cannot
love
      back

on breaking you

i'm sorry
for everything i've ever done
to you

know that
it was not the me
i
want to be
that
made
me do it

one-woman-man

i long to be
a one-woman-man
fused together, cheek-to-cheek
lost within
our own mystique

your spectral eyes piercing
        mine
like daggers in a medieval battle
in full view
        of the sun's deceit

and i long to hold you
forever
        maybe longer
though i know
someday my bones will turn
to dust
my eyes will grow heavy
in life, then death, and maybe
then in life again –
        50, 60, 70 years
1000 years
if only i could

our outstretched hands, in life
then death, and maybe in life
again
entwined
like olive branches growing
together towards the sun
      the same sun that creeps into
your basement studio
you, all perfect skin and optimism
sculpting clay
into near-flawless
      living forms

      it's my masterpiece, you whisper
with enchanting breasts
      pressed
   firmly
against
   revealing lilac

      but you are the masterpiece, i say
and i mean it
though you don't hear;
      the moment lost forever
though the thought
imprinted
in a mind still dreaming

of
being a one-woman-man.

my phone vibrates
and it's her again, a zealous guest
for willing men
and i just can't help myself

open message

download attachment

a fine body
transparent panties
the promise of a tidy fix
and
        there i am again
the trance
brooding in my loins
seeping through my resolution
a silent sexual
        revolution
and like
a poison my body
cannot fight
the urge to fuck comes over me

a hurricane
                inside my brain
i feel the rise
                an infection
my immunity has no antibodies for
        my mind
has no resistance to; zero defence
in the face of a malignant
force

i make my excuses
leave
              but what about your masterpiece?

stomping through lofty grass
towards
another faceless, loveless
fuck
all sweat and gristle and gracelessness
no roses, movies
compliments
nothing –
just question-less morbidity
        pressed against
un-plastered walls

no
pleasantries to finish; a silent, hurried
    wipe
on scraps of kitchen paper
avoiding eyes
always avoiding eyes

    i'll be in touch

    sure, she groans, cigarette in hand

the
    cinders
        falling
to
the plastic lino
ashen snowflakes in deep
december

and i'm back
on the pathways through the parkways
through dimly-lit
alleyways
the reverberations of my
guilt-ridden secretion pounding
in my temples
the aftershocks of seismic

desire
pouring from my brain
hot liquid
into my glands
my nodes, my organs, my rationale
into my will
every inch of my
being;
a shameful
      six-second miracle
breathless foil for satisfaction
wicked-hot
            chain reaction
a primitive evacuation
of
lust

emptiness

a solitary candle, barely lit
floating
      in the wildest oceans
lost

      how was your day? you whisper

head
on my chest, weaving the hairs
around your
fingertips

                and i'm back
                  a one-woman-man
again

isn't that just like
        me?

sorry

i guess in truth
i always
knew

you fell for
         a lover
that couldn't
be true

total control

i conduct
the orchestra
    of your misery
and
i hate myself
for
    it

encore

when the curtain rose
there was only
you
just left
      of centre
pale grey eyes

solitary applause
from the boy
who
      for so long
claimed
to be a man

who for so long
failed
      to be anything
to you
      at
all

remedy

i want to
get
        drunk

but i know
i will
        wake
to
the horror
        of my own words

in the end

i swallow
your compliments
like
shards
      of glass
and
spit them out
when
      you turn your back

it's
just the way
we've
      come to be

don't be surprised

if
i disappoint
you

it's the only thing i know

the fear at the back of my mind

maybe
      i am dying

because
      these words are
spilling out
like a flood
i
cannot control

three

female of the species

in time

i saw her sing
the opera

        emerging
from the shadows
like
a full force gale

    and
it felt like
  epic
glorious death

her
huge waistline
        violently shaking
with each courageous
    note;
the thunderous quake of
      her lungs
    my ears
a fleck of
turquoise mascara

Paul Robert Mullen

trickling
        down
                her
                        ageing
                                cheek
the only escapee
in
        a room
                of four thousand

Shakespeare wrote the most notable tragi-comedy

scaling the city streets
of hong kong
looking for a cheap beer
at dusk
scurrying through the rancid smell
of grilled tofu
steaming on the greasy
hot plates of street vendors
masked, desensitised
overworked
and down on their luck.

    "hey, sir, come in!" she bellows
flying
out of a doorway somewhere, anywhere
i don't know
like an unexpected moth
that flits
    around your face

    "we got girls and girls and girls!"

grabbing at my elbow
hanging on for dear life

    "no!" i remonstrate

trying to walk into city lights
    and the stench
the immovable mass of
blank faces
rushing in and out of fine rain

    "come on, come *on!*"
she pleads
yanking at my sleeve
my indecision
pulling me, pushing me
holy shit, woman
retching, moaning
kicking, screaming
like a puppy
at the heels with insane grip

    "i don't *want* to," i insist
trying
to shake free
to return to the rain in peace, but she

won't have it
this slightly heavy filipina
in ill-fitting glitter
sequined, stretched
fit to burst

    "what you drink?"

wild-eyed
ready to get into it
a terrifying hunk of
womanhood
a female spider luring me
to the web
to the plate

    "beer!"
i react
(stupidly)

    "you come!"
heaving me
bending me out of shape
licking my skinny ass into this
impossible eventuality
through the door

"you drink first beer free!"

and i'm through the curtain
kidnapped, overwhelmed
damp from the trials of the street, staring at
an empty room – a solitary flashing
light strobing the twisted faces
of a million ageing girls, stripped to their lace
and their cellulite and their misery

"you drink! you drink!" she laughs
nest
of cockroach smile, handing me
a dusty bottle of shit beer
no english label. i take a swig
drinkable
(maybe)

"hey!" someone shouts
and
there she is
queen kong herself, eyeing me from
the shadows of a stale booth
and my neck is starting to sweat, my stomach
turn somersaults. the realisation
that i am the only man in there
the only chunk of fresh prey, the door now blocked

by half a dozen
enormous silhouettes
torn faces and snake-skin
cravings

    "you sit!" she points
and i do
since my options are limited
and my beer only half empty
she's a big girl
big enough to shake the seas
not a day under forty
hunched from years of meaningless fucks
stooped with the weight of
gargantuan tits
the rejections, humiliations

    "i've got biggest titties in here!"
she motions
peeling her bra down
to the roof of her nipples, pressing them together
and i squirm
at the thought of it all
the very sadness
and indignity of it all

    "i'm really not …"

        "shut up!" she scowls. "you just like rest come here!"

        "no, no . . ."

        "you motherfuck shit! you rat man!
                    beer and fuck, fuck and beer!
                            you want the titties!
            you want drink beer while fuck me!
                        you filth shit! you dirt!"

sneering
thrusting her finger at me
accusing me

        "no, no, you got it all wrong!"

        "i tell you something," she leans in
                        confidential
tits pressed together again
with the insides of her wrists; two mountains
in a sea of strobe
                    light
swirling
around a vacant floor

> "nobody gets out here alone!
>
>   may as well take me!"

rush of nausea
stinging gut

the communards,
                don't leave me this way . . .
but
nobody there to get down

    "i'm not interested!" i insist

    "you better be!"

    "*what?*" incensed

    "dumbass!" she screams

i scan the room, looking for
an exit; nothing. entrance
blocked. the mistress
bringing more beer. i'm a centipede
            bent over by
an elephant; all the legs
in the world
no use.

i sense
the other girls getting restless
watching
waiting
      for their chance
to pounce

      "i like you," she whispers

"holy *shit*!"

      "you take me home, foreign man!"

"no!"

      "fucking dumbass!" she wails
slugging at the beer
that i'd apparently bought

some other
poor bastard gets shoved through
the door
      equally as shocked
equally
as appalled
and i wonder whether hell
has come to claim me

early;
>	death's door-handle
in my hand
a bush fire in my temples

a limp cock.

>	"i wait no man," she spits. "pay bill, we *go*."

"wait, wait," i shudder
manic
>	buying time
"you've not even told me your name."

the strobe looping
the other guy squirming
two caught in the web; a mad, sad
battle
for the buffet.

>	"me? *name?*"

"yes," i plead, trying to straighten
>	all this out.

>	"thunder-cunt."

"*what?*"

"thunder-*cunt*!"

"*thunder-cunt?*"

"you got it, gringo!"

Barry White.
i mean, Barry White in a den full of
spirit suckers, murderers
jizz-theives

"don't you have a real name?"

"that *is* real name!" snarling

"you must have a *rea*l name – like leslie, or amy
or mary, or something?"

"thundercunt!"

more beer. i wave it away.
they insist. i shout, stand up to my
full height
               teetering
staggering

wavering on the edge

"thundercunt, i am leaving."

      "you go nowhere, silly foreign man!"
all gums
and crooked teeth
thrusting her foot into my crotch
pinning me
         to the seat

"please," i jitter

    "now, to your home!" she demands

"oh, *shit* . . ."

walking the soaking streets
the looks from passers-by burning into my pores
    into my eyes
they know the score
know exactly
where we're going
what we're doing
        and she clinks and clanks
in her high heels
until enough is enough

                        plucking
them off, linking my arm
tip-toeing
with the delicacy of a herd
            of elephants
through
steaming rat-shit-puddles
        into
                the worst nightmare
                i've ever had
                        the misfortune
                                of detailing in a poem.

dream catcher

she has eyes
like
troubled dreams

        and
i hang on
the
walls, grasping for something

    anything
everything
        nothing

the cat
    sleeps through it all

subtle rubble

there was a weed growing
within our love
    (probably) for years

    twisting itself
around my veins
stemming the flow
       of blood
to my brain, pulling
me away
from all i knew, from all i thought
    i wanted to know

it burrowed into other peoples' lives
so deep
       underground
it weaved
and wretched
    and strangled
the love from
my heart

by the time i snapped free
    you

were already gone.

you want to know
the truth?

i don't blame you

requiem for the lovers

when i walked into the pub
i felt the sudden glare
of glassy eyes. she'd seen me
come in. through my peripheral
antennae
        i'd seen her too

the fire roared, the jukebox
swayed with 70's soul
the vinegary smell of stale booze
fermenting the air, and the voices of those
            present and past
dancing on the eternal
sound waves
            that permeate
our
fragile, sheet-glass
minds

"is that the Average White Band?" someone asked
            yes, my mind replied

it was the day we lost
another rock star; three in a week

another name
off the shelves of middle-class
homes
      consigned to memory

she strained to look
                as i waited at the bar
but halted when our eyes
threatened
to meet. that agonising
                post-sex-depression
the bones in her face
restructuring as the minutes
melted into hours, booze moulded our
conspicuous histories
the flames, mid-tango, swirling
twisting, retching
        in their voodoo
        ritual

i took my seat by the fire
appropriately shadowed, next to a crowd
of younger girls
      barely legal
speaking of period pains
and big cocks, pecs, travel insurance
lingerie

a freezing cold december eve
alone by the fire
a crowded room
        alone.

i watched through semi-steamed, leaded
    windows. the streets
      bubbled; tension, as the hoodies
of a provincial town loitered
giving edge to
      a fading dusk
waiting for their moments
      of glory
for their piece of the action
and all that time
    she never stopped that solid
      stare
from the comfort of her
cotton-clad, bacardi-breathed nest
i could feel it, like a spider
on my neck
the occasional nip, the threat
of the bite
      how much more can i tolerate?
wracked
by the memory

        of my own mistakes
calling on my demons
to let me go

each time i returned to the bar
dry, in limbo
the landlady studied me more
fixed upon the bloodshot eyes, the imminent
tears, the vulnerability
in my voice. each time, with greater
reluctance
she watched me back to my corner, drink in hand
      the night running away with the
        howling winds and the wine and the shot-gun
thoughts
of hopelessness
the blurred visions of surviving
a plane crash
being lost at sea –
              the sickening
realisation of violence
the
constant, futile struggle
      of simply waiting for God

the christmas spirit
was upon us, amongst us; glasses clinked

hands were shaken
and i recalled that final text
       of hers:

  **i've grown because of what you did to me
    not what you did for me**

  and i scrutinised
the people getting leery, consumed by
the night, by the things
they'd bought
things
   that nobody needs
with money
nobody has
to impress people
nobody even likes

and the wine
it was pulsing in my head
the cracks in the city opening up wide
before me
the howls of death
    or worse
on the streets outside, calling like
a timekeeper
smoke as bitter as sour milk

and the whiskey and the wine and the resentment
of being on the losing end
the confusion of it all
desire versus compromise
now versus forever

is my future locked inside my past?

the bell rings

it's nearly
        over
one
last stand –

from the corner of one quietly closing eye
the nest
splits

time
    for farewells, best wishes
      community
          insincerity
the careless hugs of strangers
the
short-back-and-sides prescription bespectacled
professionals full of blow

and dark ideas
the girls full of impossible dreams

and
    mine

fur coat
    in hand

so near and yet so far
preparing my latest
devastation
with the calmness
    of a warm
  dusk

seasons

you started out as
spring –
        a foreboding beauty
blossoming
in late march
        rains

you became
        summer – burning
bright within me
upon me
my hand to hold in
        the darkness of
        my dreams

but autumn came; you withered
a little
started to bend away
        from the light that gave us
life

winter was the death
        of us –
you

frozen unrecognisable
only ice
in the rare
        embraces
            left

separation

my brain, your brain
explode
    like confetti
shatter
    like spider-webbed
    dreams
detonates
    the ugliness within

surrounded by
the things that everyone else
wants for us
the visions of what
everyone else needs from us

    60-inch plasma
    alloy wheels
    surround sound stereo system
        stainless-steel-
            coffee-maker
the
never ending
    conciliations

for a void
the universe
 could never fill

don't

when you come to visit me in my one-up one-down
please don't bring your pearls. i will make the tea and the
conversation no doubt, and you will make amends.

i brush my teeth with colgate these days. i look for it
in the offers. sometimes the leaflet comes
through my door – we're a target area for the
common-man-supermarkets, you see. discount salami,
hunks of dutch cheese, potato chips, bread sticks with dips,
tinned sardines – a treat for the dog. so please
don't park your z-series on my front when
you come. take the bus. it will do you good to see how
the other half live. and please, don't quote f.scott fitzgerald
when you are telling me about your kids.
he was a drunk anyway.

please don't turn your nose up at my carpets, scoff at my
choice of colour. don't tell me that wooden floors
are 'in' now – i have no interest in hip, and cannot afford them
regardless. do not shake your head as you peruse
my records, my books, my movies, my life.
just don't do it.

please don't insist on explaining yourself again. don't tell me

that i changed, pushed you away, made you feel lonely,
estranged.

don't tell me that you fucked him
because i kept all my love for myself.
don't tell me that i caused this
      when you couldn't understand my love
over gold.

don't lay your burdens at my door. the truth
resides in our own entangled histories, but it is no longer
my cross to bear.
      i am clean.

don't hold your cappuccino with extended
little finger – you are not
      the Queen.

and one last thing. don't paint my afternoon with solemn
colours
when i am here willing to forgive.

do you hear?
just *don't*.

you

I.

remind me of the way
love could be
         should be

you take me back
to a time when love was real
when the union
of hearts was more than just
mediocrity
      vanity
            the promise of safety
    convenience
keeping
up with the jones's
the needs and desires and aspirations of others
exuberance
face
shambolic immaturity
                  lies
you remind me
that none of this
      matters

II.

      are
the
glorious metaphor
that
      means something new
every time
our
      eyes
            meet

III.

hold me
hostage
in
     my
own
     dreams

IV.

take my breath
      away
but
you give me
      so much more
in
return

V.

decorate
my days
with a gloss you cannot
buy in
      shops

you
        infiltrate
my smile
with edges that i
   cannot fake

when
        morning rouses me
your smell
takes me to places
i cannot go alone

you
     are

childhood

i can smell your father
on you
      cigarette smoke and bare knuckles
         imprinted on your veins

when i hold you
you
      cannot hold me
      back
since
the years have deprived you
of trust

when i smile
at you
your face aches in ways i've never seen

underneath it all
you
      want to mimic me
though
      you don't know what it
      really means
         to smile

i
see
promise
in the first light of dawn
but
  all you see
is another day to endure

yet
  the miracle
    is this:

whenever i walk away

    you follow

the worst night of my life

it was the night of the
great monsoon
and i couldn't get my kicks
so i rang
the hotline and she arrived
soaking wet, shivering through
her plastic mac
so i brought her in, wrapped her
in a towel
made us both a mad-dog
      margarita

she was in the shower
before long. i could hear that rasping
cough – a churning, guttural heaving
from the base of her
              tiny breasts
and my hard-on
went limp
my mind began
to sober
and the rains battered my windows like a mocking crowd
sensing my regret

she came out of the bathroom
                         withered, naked
ready to face her latest
impassive slump
detached, skeletal love. no amount
of sucking could give me a rise

       i was already dying inside
       she was already dead

and the tears came, abandoned shakes
lips trembling
pride disintegrating. she curled up
in a ball, foetal, destitute
       head resting on my wilted dick
weeping for every hooker
that ever waited in the shadows
for their kids'
three square meals a day

       we lay for the longest hours
i'd ever had, and the rains
       eased
the dawn light tiptoed in unannounced
and i put her fee
on the table next to my father's
tobacco box, made in india. we shared a cigarette

Guy Clark singing softly
        on the early morning country-music broadcast
and she left
wounded
without word
dragging herself into the blinding
half-light
     to the tune of freighters
          docking nearby

i showered and showered
     scrubbing and scrubbing and *scrubbing*
under boiling water
my skin smelling
of rotting meat
a puritanical lust for my own
virginity
behind
the fierce scratching
of blunted nails, trying desperately to
rip her stench
   from my pores
from my memory
the sickly stale saliva
clinging to my dick, making me
wretch
wretch

clinging to me
despite the soap

the news said
that the storm had taken eight people
thirty-two were missing
hundreds injured
though a small dog, a daschund i think
had made it through
the gales; something
                            to hold on to
at least.

the carcass of a
twenty-three year old staring back
at me in the mirror
the bulletin unfolding on the sound waves
and the hookers
                hoping for beautiful, foolish arms
striking deals with
empty shells, like me, on street
corners
      in that drowning city

of dreams

little joan

she had a ton of fish
        the colour of the rainbow
a stylish coat rack
        (parisian i'd guessed)
and a stack of
Hemingway on a crystalline coffee table
        untouched

she offered a mocha
        with a hint of ginger
i said it was late
she poured anyway

        "you know, you should aspire
                to be happy," she maintained

twisting her forefinger
around a loose hem on her
mauve velvet coat, looking me over
        with eyes demanding
            hope
she
pulled and pulled
without success, slumped into a georgian

leather chair
lit up

she pushed her smokes across
the coffee table. i pushed
them back

there was design
       behind the stand off
and
       i never did
       like that chair

infatuation

watching 4am descend
once more
like
      a bad memory

watching her
waltzing through stone
with the touch
of a stranger

and
i know now
why love takes more courage

      than laughter

departure

i don't hold you
to
    stop you leaving

i hold you
so
    you can guide me
wherever
    you go

four

temporary lights

return of the muse

my pen
       exploded
on the
harbours of hong kong

one-hundred floors
       of fierce steel peering
       at me
from
all sides

       but

only
the sun
       from above

long after the war

sometimes in dreams i wake
in russia, striped by venetian blinds as

bell boys rush through the corridors
of your conscience. i'm consumed by the forgotten laughter

of the 1980's – the silhouette of 1987 etched
on the rising curtain, relieving me

of darkness; a solitary creature emerging slowly
from the shadows of the balustrade

"the show," you motion, pointing at the sadness
in the eyes of the singer

"of course," i smile

pretending to care. the rains welcomed us later
as midnight crept near like an over-sexed

alley-cat, scratched and scarred from the tantric battles
of the night

shall i do it anyway?

the
        poetry
i really
want to write
i
cannot write

i
fear
        that one day
you might
read it

Paul Robert Mullen

voodoo sound

is it still
       a poem
if
all i say
       is

nothing
makes me feel the way i feel
when
       i hear
the refrain
in
       Gimme Shelter?

call it wonder

i am enchanted
by
    the aluminium
             white dove
that
takes me to places
i never
thought
      i'd see

i am not alone in this battle

i was sat reading a poem by Ginsberg
my feet dangling over
      the edge of the world

in it he said
      someday i'll be dead

and now he's dead

so where is he now?
how does he feel?
was death really so painful?
what is it like to live
foretell
die?

i think about that one
solitary moment of death – a tiny fragment
in the vast epic moments of
      life

sometimes i dream
      that i am dreaming
sometimes i chase down the years

      like a rabid wolf, but when i get there
      i can't remember why
sometimes i step outside myself
      and scream
sometimes i loiter where shore meets shore
      waiting for Marlene Dietrich
      or God
           or somebody

sometimes i perish
beneath the weight of happiness
sometimes i dangle
      by a broken thread hanging
      from your eyes
sometimes i pick my pride up from the gutter
      and place it in shop windows
           illuminated
      by temporary lights

often, i will suffocate
      inside the pores of your skin

sometimes i will just
      be

five

street life

aftermath

"love is everything we said it wasn't"
—*Charles Bukowski – a definition*

the honey slides down my
parched throat
gracefully, mid-speed
like a snake over
sand

tell me something real, you said

so i will

sat here, listening to Nat King Cole
staring at an ex-lover. i'd like to
fuck her again
but i never want to see her again

is that honesty enough?

maybe
i will kill her
in my dreams. maybe i will
fuck her in
my nightmares or my sunday best

maybe Nat will be drowned out by my
silent musings

there are black clouds hanging
over my domain. she wears shades
to cover the shame

i'm
lying here, almost vertical
poisoned by
an irrational lust
             that thumps at my constitution
like an african drum

maybe i will die
             tonight
maybe she will
read the eulogy; tear it up
toss it into the flames with the shell
of my being

the perfect ending to a
perfect tragedy

the song changes. Tony Bennett.
he left his heart in san francisco. i left mine between

her salivating jaws, and she *bit*
shark speed
lion strong
        so hard

i took myself to the other side
of the world, watched
some movies, wrote some poems
laced my despair with a shot of fake indifference

        nobody knew!

nobody knew.

i'd been slowly charred by my vision
of completeness
        until the heat came over me tenfold
        began to spittle all around me
        pop, crackle, melt me
they
didn't know i'd had my heart
        surgically removed by a waitress;
            no anaesthetic
            no tenderness
            no warning

she thinks i still care, that i still want her

but you see
i no longer have the heart
to care
my breath like iron
only the raging, soulless craving
to fuck

i am a bear post-hibernation
      i am a cockroach in its swarming cesspool
           heaven
      i am the shark devoid of motive
      i am the ghost in the machine
      i am the story teller hiding behind the syllables
      i am the porn star
           balls deep
      i am the vengeance in a thousand smiles
      i am the shocked emoji
           in your final message
      i am a law unto myself

if i am lucky enough for any critic
to read this
they will call me a misogynist
a madcap
      or worse

maybe even sociopath:

this is not poetry! this is not art!
this is the ravings of a lunatic!
this is obscene!
don't encourage it!
don't read it!

it's getting harder to blame her
      for leaving

the song changes. Eva Cassidy.
boy, do i believe her
when she sings. i hang on her every pained
expressive word
she fills me with the kind of joy
that no woman, flesh or bone, here and now
could ever do

      i've still the mind to feel without
      the heart
      to love

somewhere over the rainbow
the skies are blue
and i believe her Lord, i do.
but where?
where do i need to go?
where is this rainbow? the blue skies?

Paul Robert Mullen

you see, the trouble with this life
is
    that it's always
        somewhere
        somehow
        someday
  never
        here
        now
        today

the coffee house is my
sanctuary. it is proving my sanity. my stability
the place where death
        doesn't exist

that's where i'll go

the restfulness, the comings and goings
the innocent individual intimations
the restfulness, the melting together
    all together, all alone
the well-earned
        break
the serendipity
the sweet, sobering coffee. i'm glad she's gone now

without an encore
no sequel, no low-budget reprise

i'm back to my
glorious loneliness
in amongst a room of broken hearts
        slowly dying
but dying in peace
books in hand, pens in the throes
of future masterpieces

and it doesn't matter
what the song is anymore

on donald trump

i urge
        everyone
to
believe in
whatever they believe
                in

just
face the consequences
      with
           grace

vanity

otherwise
> known as

    SELFIE

death of society

the streets are
a tragedy. nobody talks to each-
    other
nobody greets strangers. nobody smiles
to help me through my day
nobody
asks about
    the weather
nobody
stops to help
nobody looks up
    to take in the
magnificence

all of these
hearts
    and lives
trapped
within a
    3 by 6 inch
    screen

whoever keeps taking them took him too

there are black holes
swallowing
        the stars
one-by-one

        leaving my skies
bare
like the soles
on a pair of worn-out
    shoes

the kind you find
in a
      second-hand
store

a mediocre journey

the train station
is desperately cold. a shivering platform
waiting to embark
a lone raven circling the rafters,
        lost.
a disabled man, riddled with the frustrations
of a thousand centuries
tinnitus, loneliness
crowded by able but unwilling legs

        "this is not delicious!" a child screams
all
hair lip and fury
flashing in my eyes.

Dvorak, Monteverdi, Tchaikovsky,
Bach. i've heard them all. they took shit from the gutters
and the hospitals and the rat-infested
churches, the madhouses and the prisons
and the school bullies
and they made it shine

i read Miller as a kid, Beckett as a man
Celine when i begged for death

Bukowski when
        confronted with life
i swam for my county
reeled at pictures of the war. made myself sick in unlit
parkways with
cheap cider and weed
cursed at the moon
dipped my fingers into
the knickers
of a thousand dirty dreams

        "what did you say?" somebody said
somehow to *me*
though i faked disinterest
choosing to sip my coffee
inhale the breeze
disappear into the firework voices exploding
from the office blocks of the immoral
the depraved, the lost
and found (as detailed on the inner pages
of my tattered tourist guide – broken spine, bereft of
the line)

"wake me on the other side," she whispered
        so loudly

that the earth shook
and the heavens stood still

only the fly on
the wall
    moved
off
into the ether
to report its unlikely
    tale

street life

is
the stray
with
a broken leg
dragging itself
defeated
to the
        gutter
to die

six

spinning crimson

welcome the morning

open the blinds

      go on, open them just
          a little

give my bones a chance
      to grow

give my skin a chance
      to heal

give my eyes a break
      from the dark, for they are
      stinging
heavy

give my dreams the chance
        to manifest
in daylight

and
your arms, my arms

the chance
> to reach

for
> the sun

hindsight

i've stopped opening my mouth
these days
because
my words
light fires in all
the
        wrong places

instead
i write it all down
on
pages like these

                you see
i've found with age
that
        my pen
puts
           fires out
where
spoken words

        ignite

Paul Robert Mullen

sunlight on the windscreen

i miss walking down the pier-head
in winter
past
beer-maddened
tramps and weary
housewives pushing grandchildren
full of screams
      eager for air

i miss the rattle
of the inter-city against the backdrop
of the dunes, rolling
tears and fears and memories
away from their
versions
of truth

i miss the rains
thundering in from the irish sea
      the sweet taste
of strawberry summers – whipped cream
and caramel; the reflection
of the marina
      at midnight

after the movies have dribbled our young imaginations
back onto the streets
and the ethereal
thudding
of this teenage heart
        as soaking wet ideas awoke me
                from adolescence

i miss the fledgling thought that
love can be
a lasting treasure

i miss
the hypnotic commotion
of the turntable
                in full flow
spinning crimson
in a room full
of greens and blues

i miss you
                too
and
don't you just
                know it

avalon revisited

the fields rolled out before us
caterpillar green
carpeting the horizon

courage
   doesn't come easy

it weaves its way
through thorns and rattlesnake reveries
through the quick-sands
      that suck our seconds away
         strangle our ambition, poison our
            tenacity

we packed our bags and
made our way
        to the gates
and though i was ashamed
that my nails were bitten to the core
and the callouses
     lining my palms were hard
        ugly
     she smiled, asked for
my hand;

        we walked on
towards our horizon
two worlds colliding
          because
that was how
it was meant
          to be
regardless
of
the atom bomb
and
the cries of the inevitable

wasted on the way

making the grade

maybe
i was born with
    the inability to give
back what i have
selflessly
    been given
in a life
where we are measured
by what we
    can give
and not
    how much
we
    can love

seven

follow me

the reasons

i have not entered
this life
       simply to survive

i want to smell it
i want to feel it
i want my thoughts
              to fly
miles above the
       hours and days and years
       and generations
              spent
wading through bloodied
       gory
shitty wastelands

i want to trust my leaders

i want to see
insignia
in the landscapes stretched out before me
not the lifeless
       greys
that

bury me before
                i'm dead

i want the churches of
my homeland
to fill me with the will
                to believe

i want to see your smile
behind the agony
                of it all

will you follow me
                if i promise
we can see
        whatever we want to see

together?

my only idea

let us take
        our terror
our mischief
our lust for life
        all around the world
and
bleed ourselves dry
until
        all the fun
                we have
kills us

my only idea

eight

curtain call

conviction

"i'm not looking for miss right,"
                he said.

"i'm looking for miss *tonight*."

acknowledgements

I'd like to thank my parents and my sister, and my grandparents, alive and passed, for always being a solid foundation in my life. Kate Evans for the inspirational weekly meetings in a certain coffee shop in Nanning, China. Fran Zinder and Dave Rhine for listening. Jan McCutcheon for another great design, and tireless editing from across continents. The late and beyond great Leonard Cohen for opening doors in my mind I'd never imagined were even there. The noises in the walls, the wild-eyed wanderers of the world, and Mother Nature for her epic sub-tropical storms that forced me to stay home and write.

Thanks to whoever invented cheese and red wine.

Paul Robert Mullen was born in Southport,
near Liverpool, England, in 1982.
He is a writer, musician, and University Lecturer,
currently living and working in Nanning, Guangxi, China.
His poetry has been widely
published in a variety of literary journals,
magazines and e-zines. He is also an avid blogger.

He is the author of *curse this blue raincoat* (2017)

www.mushythebeatle.wordpress.com
www.mushythebeatle.blogspot.be
fb.me/PaulRobertMullenWriter
author.paul.mullen@gmail.com

www.ingramcontent.com/pod-product-compliance
Lightning Source LLC
Chambersburg PA
CBHW070449050426
42451CB00015B/3400